T H I S   B O O K
B E L O N G S   T O

soulmaker | PRESS

Soulmaker Press
soulmakerpress.com

Cover design by Liliana Guia

ISBN: 978-1-961064-26-3

VOLUME ONE

THE
EROS SUTRAS

workbook

Principles

NICOLE DAEDONE &
AUBREY FULLER

CONTENTS

INTRODUCTION
WELCOME TO YOUR JOURNEY
INTO THE EROS SUTRAS

This journey is completely yours, from the pace you set to the depths you go. Whether you prefer to take your time and deeply immerse or move swiftly through, this workbook is designed to be your companion as you explore the foundations of the Eros philosophy. As you embark, it's essential to have *The Eros Sutras, Volume 1: Principles* by your side. Within these pages, you'll find ample space to journal your thoughts and answer questions that will guide you deeper into the Sutras, making this experience uniquely yours.

This workbook is structured to encourage a sequential journey through *The Eros Sutras: Volume 1: Principles*, the bedrock of the path of Eros. By engaging with the questions provided, you're invited to not just casually read and observe but to intimately connect with each Sutra, stepping inside your understanding and interacting with them for a deeply personal experience. These inquiries are designed to draw you closer to the essence of each Sutra, allowing for a shift in perception that opens the doors of your interior world to a more profound connection with yourself and the world around you.

As you progress through the workbook, the questions become catalysts for self-discovery, prompting reflections that may reveal aspects of yourself and life that you haven't yet ventured into. This process is not simply about intellectual growth but awakening your Erotic mind, a shift in consciousness that is a stark contrast to rational thought. The Erotic mind can see into the workings of the interior of life where the rational mind remains on the outer edges, knocking at doors closed to tourists. These doors only open for an inquiring consciousness that desires to be truly touched and changed by experience.

This is more than a guide; it's a gateway to developing an Erotic way of seeing and feeling, inviting you to engage with life from an entirely new perspective. Its interactive design will create a dynamic portrait of your internal path as you work through the Sutras, a "you are here" moment at the beginning of your journey on the Erotic path.

A Bit More about the Eros Sutras

The Eros Sutras are a collection of teachings on the philosophy of Eros. Drawing from the Sanskrit word *sutrā*, referring to spiritual or philosophical teachings, *The Eros Sutras* serve as a guide to exploring the mystical state, where people learn to be fully themselves and live a life based in connection and truth.

The Sutras are a map to how our minds work, offering instruction and insight for how to live a more fulfilled and connected life. The Sutras describe how to approach life with an open heart and mind through the complexities of human relationships and the pursuit of personal liberation. They offer a unique and compelling perspective on seeing and engaging with the world.

The philosophy described in *The Eros Sutras* helps individuals understand how the world works and how people interact with it and within it. The Sutras show that there is a possibility for a different way of life, tapping into the often-overlooked or misunderstood aspects of existence, like Erotic energy, feminine wisdom, and the knowing of the body. These principles offer insights into how one can work with life's natural rhythms and energies, allowing us to navigate challenges with grace, deepen our connections with others, find joy in the everyday, and lead a life of flourishing.

Ultimately, *The Eros Sutras* invite us to rewild our nature and rediscover the joy and connection that come from living in resonance with ourselves and the world. They open the possibility for a more vibrant, connected, and fulfilling life, grounded in the truth and aligned with the deeper currents of existence.

The first volume of *The Eros Sutras*, to which this workbook is the accompaniment, establishes the basis for sensing, following, and tuning in to the force of Eros. The reader is introduced to the Erotic perspective of perfection, desire, interdependence, optionality, play, ethics, and more.

PERFECTION

1.

ALL IS PERFECT WITH ROOM TO EVOLVE

- ◆ Have you ever felt obligated to see reality as broken or to see the world as terrible?

_____

_____

_____

_____

_____

_____

- ◆ How are the senses tied to perceiving perfection? Do you allow yourself to fully immerse in your senses?

_____

_____

◆ Was there any part of the Sutra that relieved any burdens you have been carrying?

_____

_____

_____

_____

_____

_____

◆ What is one pattern/flaw you have that you can see at times serves a valuable purpose?

_____

_____

_____

_____

_____

2.

BEING WITH THINGS
AS THEY ARE

◆ When was the first time you remember feeling
pressured by an outside source to design your life in a
particular way or to achieve a specific goal or to become
a certain kind of person?

_____

_____

_____

_____

_____

_____

◆ What is one place in your life where you have been really hard on yourself about being something you are not? Is there a place where you can admit you can't force yourself to do that, where you can't quite fit the mold?

_____

_____

_____

_____

_____

_____

3.

PERFECTION,
NOT PERFECTIONISM

◆ What was a moment in your life when things were really hard and you rose to the occasion?

_____

_____

_____

_____

_____

_____

◆ What is an emotion or experience that you tend to bypass instead of have intimacy with because it is painful?

_____

_____

_____

_____

_____

_____

◆ Where is a place in your life where you have tried to create a "movie-scene perfect" outcome?

_____

_____

_____

_____

_____

_____

◆ What does resting in perfection mean to you?

_____

_____

_____

_____

_____

_____

4.

APPROVAL

◆ How does approval summon forth the nobility in us?

_____

_____

_____

_____

_____

_____

◆ Why is it that we can really only practice approval when
we are rooted in our own sense of perfection?

_____

_____

_____

_____

_____

_____

♦ What is one thing you thought was only ugly but then you found something sublime in?

_____

_____

_____

_____

_____

_____

♦ What is the difference between approval and acquiescence and how do they feel different?

_____

_____

_____

_____

_____

_____

5.

PERFECTION RESTORES US

◆ Have you ever encountered someone in an ungratifiable mindstate? What was that like?

_____

_____

_____

_____

_____

_____

◆ How is it actually helpful to your own life and the people around you if you perceive yourself as perfect, just as you are?

_____

_____

_____

_____

_____

_____

◆ What would development of a mature Erotic mind look
like to you?

_____

_____

_____

_____

_____

_____

DESIRE

6.

A SENSORY ORGAN

◆ Did you ever have a desire that got squeezed out by an idea about what is right or appropriate? When?

_____

_____

_____

_____

_____

_____

◆ Why do you think the condition of our relationship with desire can be gauged by how fluid our body feels? Why does desire relate to the senses so much?

_____

_____

_____

_____

_____

_____

◆ Why do you think gratification can only occur when we
  serve desire rather than mere satisfaction when we have
  desire serve us?

_____

_____

_____

_____

_____

_____

7.

DESIRE USES US

- Describe the nature of your desire as though it were an animal or a being and how you currently relate to it.

_____

_____

_____

_____

_____

_____

- Name a time you tried to control or suppress a desire but you couldn't and it had its way with you anyway.

_____

_____

_____

◆ What does authentic desire mean to you?

8.

DESIRE AWAITS
OUR ADMISSION

◆ In what ways have you dismissed, diminished,
demonized a desire?

_____

_____

_____

_____

_____

_____

◆ How might respect and care for your desire catalyze
your evolution?

_____

_____

_____

_____

_____

_____

9.

HOLDING AND MOVING

◆ Describe a place in your life right now where you feel a gap between a desire you have and attaining it. What is the feeling of the gap?

_____

_____

_____

_____

_____

_____

◆ What would it be like to allow desire to move you?

_____

_____

_____

_____

_____

_____

_____

10.

CLIMAX AND DESIRE

◆ Name ten specific places you see climax consciousness occurring in your life or in the world.

_____

_____

_____

_____

_____

_____

◆ What is a "covert benefit" of bypassing fully syncing into the moment? What do you get to not feel?

_____

_____

_____

◆ What is your current relationship to climax in sex?
How do you feel about it?

_____

_____

_____

_____

_____

◆ Why might an unsettled, unresolved sensation be a seed
to Erotic consciousness?

_____

_____

_____

_____

_____

11.

THE CALL OF DESIRE

◆ What does it mean to you to let yourself be a beginner at something? What feelings of discomfort does that bring? What feelings of relief? What feelings of excitement?

_____

_____

_____

_____

_____

_____

◆ What is something in the invisible aspect of life that you are in love with?

_____

_____

_____

_____

_____

_____

◆ Envision your life built from desire and built as art.
Describe what it looks like.

_____

_____

_____

_____

_____

_____

12.

THE TRUE VALUE
OF HUNGER

◆ How is hunger one of your greatest protectors?

_____

_____

_____

_____

_____

_____

◆ What are you like and what is your life like when you
don't feel connected to your hunger?

_____

_____

_____

◆ What is a part of you that you discarded that you're hungry to re-gather?

_____

_____

_____

_____

_____

◆ What is one way you disapprove of your hunger and see it as something to fix or heal instead of feed?

_____

_____

_____

_____

_____

13.

DUTY AND DESIRE

- What is one place in your life right now where you have a complaint? Can you trace back to the desire you had that brought that particular discontent into your life?

_____

_____

_____

_____

_____

_____

- What is one thing you often feel is burdensome that you are actually thankful for?

_____

_____

14.

COMPENSATIONS FOR DESIRE

◆ How does desire actually keep the ego right-sized?

_____

_____

_____

_____

_____

_____

◆ What is a desire you had that you deemed unacceptable? Where did the energy of that desire go instead?

_____

_____

_____

_____

_____

_____

◆ Where is one place in your life where you feel ungratifiable, where no amount of that thing would be enough?

_____

_____

_____

_____

_____

_____

15.

THE LANGUAGE OF THE BODY:
THE TEN HUNGERS

◆ Identify one specific hunger you have right now for
each of the ten hungers. What are you hungry for?

A Hunger in the Realm of Truth

_____

_____

_____

_____

_____

A Hunger in the Realm of Connection

_____

_____

_____

_____

_____

A Hunger in the Realm of Attention

_____

_____

_____

_____

_____

A Hunger in the Realm of Unconditional Love

_____

_____

_____

_____

_____

A Hunger in the Realm of Touch

_____

_____

_____

A Hunger in the Realm of Expressing Love

_____

_____

_____

_____

_____

A Hunger in the Realm of Hunting

_____

_____

_____

_____

A Hunger in the Realm of Opening the Senses

_____

_____

_____

A Hunger in the Realm of Spiritual Union

_____

_____

_____

_____

A Hunger in the Realm of Digestion

_____

_____

_____

_____

Get into relationship with them. Make a map of your hungers. If you want to fulfill them, you can.

16.

FEARS WE HAVE ABOUT DESIRE

◆ Do you ever feel you will owe something if you allow yourself to receive and enjoy?

_____

_____

_____

_____

_____

_____

◆ What do you feel when you read, "...the only thing that you owe is your reception and acknowledgment of what you receive. Nothing more"?

_____

_____

_____

_____

_____

_____

◆ Where is one place in your life where you have picked a
   substitute desire that feels safer instead of the real thing?

_____

_____

_____

_____

_____

_____

17.

TRYING TO CONTROL DESIRE

♦ Write about a specific time when you tried to control how others responded to your desire.

_____

_____

_____

_____

_____

_____

♦ What is one way you try to constrict your desire?

_____

_____

_____

_____

_____

_____

18.

DESIRE IS DEMONSTRATED BY ATTAINMENT

◆ What is one thing that keeps showing up in your life in spite of your aversion or resistance to it?

_____

_____

_____

_____

_____

_____

◆ Describe a time when you had an experience of the 'on-the-spotness' this Sutra talks about.

_____

_____

_____

_____

_____

_____

19.

DESIRE IS YOUR TRUE NORTH

◆ Describe a time when you felt the true north this Sutra talks about, "where even for a second we have felt free from the narrative mind, the confines of time, the pressures of the body."

_____

_____

_____

_____

_____

_____

- Where is one place in your life you feel like you are really aimed at your true north, and one place where you feel like you are far from it?

_____

_____

_____

_____

_____

_____

20.

THE EROTIC MIND DESTABILIZES THE HOMEOSTATIC SELF

◆ Creatively describe a scene where something powerful and chaotic and unabashed rose in the doorway that is very ordered and perfectly clean and put-together. How does the order interact with the chaos?

_____

_____

_____

_____

_____

◆ Where is one place where you feel fixated where you could un-grip a little more?

_____

_____

_____

_____

_____

_____

21.

THE EROTIC ORDER

♦ What does it mean to you to be in a relationship with
the energy of desire itself, not the object of desire,
although you are utilizing the object for the
relationship?

_____

_____

_____

_____

_____

_____

◆ If you have felt the possession gradation of desire, describe what that experience was or is like. If you haven't, write about what you think it would be like and what draws you to it and/or scares you about it.

_____

_____

_____

_____

_____

_____

HAVING LEVEL

22.

DESERVING

♦ What does it mean to you to be in your body? And
what does it mean to you to surrender to your body?

_____

_____

_____

_____

_____

_____

♦ What concealed abundance do you have?

_____

_____

_____

_____

_____

_____

◆ When has a person or a situation given you a lot that
  you then couldn't receive?

_____

_____

_____

_____

_____

◆ What do you think opening in reception means?

_____

_____

_____

_____

_____

23.

RECEPTION CONFORMS
TO HOMEOSTASIS

◆ What is something you feel is outside of your bandwidth of having?

_____

_____

_____

_____

_____

_____

◆ What is something you could soften toward to let in more?

_____

_____

_____

_____

_____

_____

◆ What are some of the excuses you say to yourself in order to contract against incoming experiences?

_____

_____

_____

_____

_____

_____

◆ Write about an experience you had where you opened to something you had resistance to. How did that feel?

_____

_____

_____

_____

_____

_____

24.

THE ONLY THING WANTED
IS A LIT-UP US

◆ What does it mean to you to create a more intimate
relationship with pain and discomfort?

_____

_____

_____

_____

_____

_____

◆ What benefits occur from "continual opening in the
face of pain"?

_____

_____

_____

_____

_____

_____

◆ When is a time in your life you experienced the
"positive-charge buildup so powerful that our attention
feels dragged" part of the Sutra?

_____

_____

_____

_____

_____

_____

25.

IDENTITY IS THE
HOMEOSTASIS OF THE MIND

◆ Make two lists of beliefs you hold. Make a 'not me' beliefs list and a 'me' beliefs list.

_____

_____

_____

_____

_____

_____

◆ What does it mean to you to hold an uncomfortable sensation in order to keep your attention steady and open?

_____

_____

_____

_____

_____

_____

◆ What comes up for you reading the line in the Sutra, "There is nothing to lose so there is nothing to protect"?

_____

_____

_____

_____

_____

_____

26.
WHEN THE MIND CONTRACTS, EXHALE

◆ Write a list of sensations that you consider "bad."

_____

_____

_____

_____

_____

_____

◆ Write a list of emotions that you consider "bad."

_____

_____

_____

_____

_____

_____

◆ What do you think about the idea that discomfort
   doesn't come from difficult external circumstances but
   rather from the way we contract against them?

_____

_____

_____

_____

_____

_____

27.

THE MEANING OF RESPECT

◆ How would you say you currently engage with your hunger?

_____

_____

_____

_____

_____

_____

◆ What does this mean to you: "Listen to the conversation that happens between our deepest yearnings and our natural environment"?

_____

_____

_____

_____

_____

_____

◆ What does it mean to you to respect your hunger?

_____

_____

_____

_____

_____

_____

28.

THREATENED BY GOOD

◆ Why is fresh goodness in our lives such a threat to the tumescent mind?

_____

_____

_____

_____

_____

_____

◆ What is a recent moment you noticed yourself "artfully evoking negative behavior" from people around you to try to manage the good coming in?

_____

_____

_____

_____

_____

_____

◆ Set a timer for 10-20 minutes and write gratitudes and
  acknowledgments of all the good you have experienced.

_____

_____

_____

_____

_____

_____

_____

_____

_____

_____

_____

_____

_____

29.

BLOWING OUT ON THE GOOD

◆ Is there a person with whom (or a place where) you had a big experience happen that you then closed to or turned against?

_____

_____

_____

_____

_____

_____

- Name a place in your life where you experienced a contraction that might actually signify a good thing happened.

_____

_____

_____

_____

_____

_____

- Go to your gratitude and acknowledgment list from page 68 and pick one thing from your list and get really specific about when that happened and how it happened and how you closed against it.

_____

_____

_____

_____

_____

_____

INTERDEPENDENCE

30.

WE ARE ALWAYS
INTERCONNECTED

◆ Now is a great time to go a little deeper in your
thoughts on intimacy. *The Eros Sutras* use the word
'intimacy' a lot and are really based in the idea of having
intimacy in all aspects of your life. What does it mean
to you to have intimacy in all aspects of your life? How
do you feel about having it? What confronts you about
it? What do you love about it?

_____

_____

_____

_____

_____

_____

◆ The Sutra says, "If we can remain in our true home, alone, interconnected, and intimate, we can always be courageous in our give and take." What does that bring up for you and mean to you?

_____

_____

_____

_____

_____

_____

31.

VULNERABILITY

- How is it that we find what we truly desire through vulnerability?

  _____

  _____

  _____

  _____

  _____

  _____

- How does vulnerability lead to liberation?

  _____

  _____

  _____

_____

_____

_____

32.
EVERYTHING WE
DO MATTERS

◆ What does it mean to you to see reality with clean eyes?

_____

_____

_____

_____

_____

_____

◆ Do you feel you tend to overvalue or undervalue your
impact on others?

_____

_____

_____

◆ What is your relationship to your own value?

_____

_____

_____

_____

_____

_____

◆ Where do you compensate for a feeling of lack of value
by either overinflating your sense of self or saying, "I
don't matter"?

_____

_____

_____

_____

_____

_____

◆ What is your go-to strategy or behavior to get out of feeling the weight of the responsibility of your impact on your environment? Do you isolate or withdraw? Do you sever connection? Do you act ashamed?

_____

_____

_____

_____

_____

_____

◆ How do you feel about it being your responsibility to discover the full expression of who you are?

_____

_____

_____

_____

_____

_____

◆ What are your excuses for not fully expressing who you
   are?

   _____

   _____

   _____

   _____

   _____

   _____

◆ What role does building resilience play in fully
   expressing who you are?

   _____

   _____

   _____

   _____

   _____

   _____

33.

RECIPROCITY

♦ What are some ways you play it cool and don't lean in fully to your life?

_____

_____

_____

_____

_____

_____

♦ Where can you let yourself "warm and melt into" your life more?

_____

_____

_____

_____

_____

_____

34.

CONSCIOUSNESS AND BODY IN COMMUNION FEELS LIKE UNCONDITIONAL LOVE

◆ Describe the power and wisdom of the body.

_____

_____

_____

_____

_____

_____

◆ What are some ways that consciousness acts superior to the body?

_____

_____

_____

_____

_____

_____

◆ What do you think about this idea of consciousness surrendering to the body and making reparations?

_____

_____

_____

_____

_____

_____

35.

THE FELT SENSE OF TRUTH

◆ Do you feel you've ever embodied your "inexorable interconnectedness"?

_____

_____

_____

_____

_____

_____

◆ What is the difference between "pumping up" and "stripping down" that the Sutra talks about? Describe an experience you've had of each.

_____

_____

_____

_____

_____

_____

◆ What does the felt sense of truth feel like to you?

_____

_____

_____

_____

_____

_____

UNCONDITIONALITY

36.

EROS IS AN INVITATION TO UNCONDITIONALITY

◆ Do you find yourself to be a rational or nonrational person and why?

_____

_____

_____

_____

_____

_____

◆ Describe how this quote from the Sutra lands for you: ". . . the capacity to accurately perceive our environment and acknowledge it with a pitch-perfect response."

_____

_____

_____

_____

_____

_____

◆ What does congruence feel like to you when you experience it?

_____

_____

_____

_____

_____

_____

37.

THE VERTICAL BRINGS US TO
EROTIC ADULTHOOD

◆ What is your current relationship to the vertical
dimension?

_____

_____

_____

_____

_____

_____

◆ What is a cherished concept or belief you hold that may
be out of alignment with your deeper nature?

_____

_____

_____

_____

_____

_____

38.

EROS HAS US MAKE CHOICES THAT FEED LIFE

♦ What is a drive you cut off that then could only happen in secrecy?

_____

_____

_____

_____

_____

_____

♦ What do you feel when reading the line, "Eros says the whole playing field is open. Nothing is off-limits"?

_____

_____

_____

_____

_____

_____

39.
EROS GUIDES THROUGH
THE FELT SENSE

♦ What do you think when reading the line, "The solution to gluttony is not restriction, it is nourishment"?

_____

_____

_____

_____

_____

_____

◆ What is your current relationship to spirituality and
sexuality?

_____

_____

_____

_____

_____

_____

◆ Describe a time in your life where you opened an Erotic
door and found depth and richness inside a challenging
situation?

_____

_____

_____

_____

_____

_____

40.
SECOND-CLASS SPIRITUALITY

◆ How do you feel seeing how the Feminine is treated as second-class?

_____

_____

_____

_____

_____

_____

◆ What parts of your Feminine are you subjecting to spiritual sexism?

_____

_____

_____

_____

_____

_____

OPTIONALITY

41.

THE HALLWAY

♦ What do the first few lines mean to you and how do you feel when reading them? "We know. We always know. But it is fun to not know."

_____

_____

_____

_____

_____

_____

♦ When was a time in your life when you were in the hallway? Describe what it was like.

_____

_____

_____

_____

_____

_____

◆ What is it like for you to linger in the potential of things? What is it like for you to choose?

_____

_____

_____

_____

_____

◆ How do you feel about admitting that you have that much volition and choice?

_____

_____

_____

_____

_____

42.

FULLNESS CUSHIONS
REACTIVITY

◆ How do you feel about leaning into what you feel
avoidance or aversion toward?

_____

_____

_____

_____

_____

_____

◆ Have you ever let yourself really feel all of the good in
your life or do you tend to focus on what is missing?

_____

_____

_____

_____

_____

_____

◆ What would it be like to let yourself fill up on the good in your life (this doesn't mean there aren't also challenges) so much that you could allow it to be a cushion of fullness?

_____

_____

_____

_____

_____

_____

43.

NOT KNOWING IS AN
HONORABLE SPOT

- ◆ How do you respond to the experience of not knowing yet? Does that make you uncomfortable? Do you feel impatient? Or are you able to allow yourself the space and experience of not knowing?

  _____

  _____

  _____

  _____

  _____

  _____

◆ How could you let yourself honor the state of not knowing more?

_____

_____

_____

_____

_____

◆ Is there any place in your past where you withdrew or hid when you were in a state of not knowing that you could now forgive yourself for?

_____

_____

_____

_____

_____

_____

44.

GRACIOUSLY OPEN AND
SURRENDER YOUR RULES

♦ What is a rule you have that, if you were honest with
  yourself, you feel like prevents you from a deeper sense
  of understanding of the truth and beauty of something?

_____

_____

_____

_____

_____

- Where is there a place in your life you could be less rigid in your rules?

_____

_____

_____

_____

_____

_____

- What does surrender mean to you?

_____

_____

_____

_____

_____

_____

45.
RESPONSES TO LOSS
OF INNOCENCE

◆ How does it feel to you knowing that there is a fresh,
untouched part of you that can always be returned to?

_____

_____

_____

_____

_____

_____

- When having a new experience, are you able to let yourself sink into it and linger, or do you find yourself rushing through it?

_____

_____

_____

_____

_____

_____

- Do you feel like your preferences—likes and dislikes—control your life? Or do you feel like you have some optionality there?

_____

_____

_____

_____

_____

_____

46.

RETURNING TO INNOCENCE
IS OPTIONALITY

◆ How do you feel about the aspect of the Sutras that is
always calling on us to return to the body?

_____

_____

_____

_____

_____

_____

◆ Are you able to allow yourself to enjoy the here and
now and be moved by life?

_____

_____

_____

_____

_____

_____

◆ What is one way you can make a choice in your life that
   brings you further into volition and agency and out of
   simply being "carried along the old grooves"?

_____

_____

_____

_____

_____

_____

47.

REAL POWER IS
IN MEETING LIFE IN
PITCH-PERFECT RESPONSE

◆ How is it thinking of your identity as "ever-dynamic"
rather than set and static?

_____

_____

_____

_____

_____

_____

◆ Share an example of a time when you let your true nature shine, even when it went against rules of appropriateness.

_____

_____

_____

_____

_____

_____

THE SPOT

48.

THE NATURE OF THE SPOT

◆ Describe a time in your life where you felt fully "on the spot."

_____

_____

_____

_____

_____

_____

◆ Describe a time in your life where you had a "gnawing sense that something is not quite right."

_____

_____

_____

♦ What are some ways you tend to compensate for not being on the spot?

_____

_____

_____

_____

_____

♦ What's the difference between seeing the truth of a particular circumstance and seeing the truth of the entire landscape?

_____

_____

_____

_____

_____

- Describe a time when you experienced a person or a situation as being beautiful and making so much sense, but in your gut, you knew something was off.

_____

_____

_____

_____

_____

_____

- Where are you willing to deviate from your own deep knowing (in order to stay comfortable, in order to stay looking good, in order to not be made a fool of)?

_____

_____

_____

_____

_____

_____

◆ Why is it more enjoyable to offer yourself fully to your life when you are on the spot?

_____

_____

_____

_____

_____

_____

49.

THE RELENTLESSNESS
OF THE SPOT

◆ What are some ways your tumescent mind speaks to
you? What are some things it says?

_____

_____

_____

_____

_____

_____

◆ How could you draw in and love your bullying
tumescent mind more?

_____

_____

_____

_____

_____

_____

◆ What is one way you are able to go inside to absorb and
  convert the tumescent mind instead of seeking for
  external comforts or soothing?

_____

_____

_____

_____

_____

_____

◆ How do you feel about the fact that the spot will ask
  everything of you at all times?

_____

_____

_____

_____

_____

_____

50.

OUR TRUEST
AND DEEPEST BEST

◆ Describe a time you felt totally "nailed."

_____

_____

_____

_____

_____

_____

◆ What is something that needs to be said in a
relationship in your life to get it back on the spot?

_____

_____

_____

_____

_____

_____

51.

THE TRUTH FULFILLS,
BUT ONLY THE TRUTH

◆ How are you at sending out and taking in? Does one
feel easier than the other?

_____

_____

_____

_____

_____

_____

◆ How does it feel when you are being moved by the
dictates of your preferences?

_____

_____

_____

_____

_____

_____

_____

◆ What does the truth feel like in your body?

_____

_____

_____

_____

_____

_____

52.
LOCK ATTENTION ON
THE DEEPER TRUTH

◆ How does it feel to think of truth as a process versus a
static thing?

_____

_____

_____

_____

_____

_____

◆ What are some ways you try to control circumstances?

_____

_____

_____

_____

_____

_____

◆ How does "the spot" and moving with the
process-oriented nature of truth relate?

_____

_____

_____

_____

_____

_____

53.

GRACE ARRIVES THROUGH HONESTY, NOT THROUGH PRETENDING

◆ Describe a place in your life where you are currently pretending or performing a state of happiness over the top of what is true.

_____

_____

_____

_____

_____

_____

◆ What does it mean to you to relate directly to this life?

_____

_____

_____

_____

_____

_____

54.

DESIRE IS THE ENERGY
OF THIS REALM

◆ How honest are you about your desires?

_____

_____

_____

_____

_____

_____

◆ What are some ways you demonize the involuntary?

_____

_____

_____

◆ What is the relationship between the spot and desire?

_____

_____

_____

_____

_____

_____

55.

TRUST IN THE TRUTH

◆ What do you think is the difference between "my truth" and the truth?

_____

_____

_____

_____

_____

_____

◆ Describe a time when you spoke the truth and something changed.

_____

_____

_____

56.

THE TRUTH DOES NOT
RESPOND TO SHOULD

◆ How do you feel about being with the fragile nature of
truth knowing also that it never goes away?

_____

_____

_____

_____

_____

_____

◆ What would you say your current relationship with
truth is like?

_____

_____

- When is a time you withheld the truth in order to manage the response of another person?

  _____

  _____

  _____

  _____

  _____

- What do you think about this line, "Truth is the currency of love"?

  _____

  _____

  _____

  _____

  _____

ELEGANCE

57.

THE EMERGENCE OF
THE INTUITIVE MIND

◆ In what ways do you find yourself tuning into the invisible, ignored, or dismissed?

_____

_____

_____

_____

_____

_____

- In what ways do you block out the invisible, ignored, or dismissed?

_____

_____

_____

_____

_____

_____

- What is your relationship to your gut sense of things?

_____

_____

_____

_____

_____

_____

◆ Have you experienced "the flood" this Sutra talks about?

_____

_____

_____

_____

_____

_____

◆ What fears come up when you think of opening more to the invisible? How concerned are you about what others may think of you if you do?

_____

_____

_____

_____

_____

_____

◆ Do you have the power to see truth and do you act on what you see?

_____

_____

_____

_____

_____

_____

58.

OUR ACCESS TO INTUITION

- What does it feel like to sink down deep below the command center of your consciousness?

  _____

  _____

  _____

  _____

  _____

- If it's true that every one of our thoughts and feelings is continually transmitted, what would you change?

  _____

  _____

  _____

_____

_____

_____

◆ What does it mean to you to have the rational mind
serve the interior world of knowing?

_____

_____

_____

_____

_____

_____

59.

UNDERSTANDINGS
ABOUT THE BODY

◆ What would it be like switching from the dictate of the
mind to separate, stabilize, and discriminate, to the
connecting, opening, and inclusion that the body
exemplifies?

_____

_____

_____

_____

_____

_____

- What is the current relationship between your mind and your body? Who do you feel like is in charge right now?

_____

_____

_____

_____

_____

_____

- What does goaless-ness mean to the body and to the mind?

_____

_____

_____

_____

_____

_____

◆ Why does the mind convince us to eject from the body?

_____

_____

_____

_____

_____

_____

◆ What does it mean to you to speak the body's language?

_____

_____

_____

_____

_____

_____

♦ What is a well-trained consciousness?

_____

_____

_____

_____

_____

_____

60.

THE EXCELLENCE
OF THE INVOLUNTARY

◆ Why can the mind bring us only to finite excellence and
not infinite?

_____

_____

_____

_____

_____

_____

◆ Why can't we fake Eros moving through our body?

_____

_____

_____

_____

_____

_____

61.

EROS SEEKS FOR THE
TOTAL EXPRESSION OF LIFE

◆ What does it mean to you to be moved by what is most
alive?

_____

_____

_____

_____

_____

_____

◆ Why do you think Eros seeks for the undifferentiated
and total expression of life?

_____

_____

_____

_____

_____

_____

◆ What is your relationship to creation and destruction?

_____

_____

_____

_____

_____

◆ Where is an unlikely place that you have found the "hallowed" presence of Eros?

_____

_____

_____

_____

_____

◆ What is something you upheld as honorable and dignified that Eros cut away?

_____

_____

_____

_____

_____

_____

EROS IS KNOWN

IMPLICITLY

62.

THE PRESENCE OR
ABSENCE OF EROS

◆ What are three other things that, when filled with Eros,
are _____, and devoid of Eros,
are _____? It can be on any
level of abstraction.

_____ when filled with Eros,
is _____, and devoid of Eros,
is _____.

_____ when filled with Eros,
is _____, and devoid of Eros,
is _____.

_____ when filled with Eros,
is _____, and devoid of Eros,
is _____.

◆ Think of an area in your life that is devoid of Eros. Describe the sensations you feel when you are in that area.

_____

_____

_____

_____

_____

_____

◆ Think of an area in your life that is filled of Eros. Describe the sensations you feel when you are in that area.

_____

_____

_____

_____

_____

_____

63.

THE GREAT WORK

◆ Who are you and who are you meant to be in this life?

_____

_____

_____

_____

_____

◆ What is one thing your interior self is asking of you that
makes you uncomfortable?

_____

_____

_____

_____

_____

_____

◆ What is something you once found unlovable in
yourself that you came to love, and something unlovable
outside of you that you came to love?

_____

_____

_____

_____

_____

_____

◆ What is one way you could offer yourself to more fully
experience life?

_____

_____

_____

_____

_____

_____

64.

INTIMACY IS THE SWEET SPOT BETWEEN MERGING AND SEPARATENESS

- What are some examples of artificial obstacles?

  _____

  _____

  _____

  _____

  _____

  _____

- How do you tend to approach your obstacles?

  _____

  _____

_____

_____

_____

_____

◆ Where do you avoid being with life on life's terms?

_____

_____

_____

_____

_____

◆ What do you think about the idea that intimate connection is a moving target, not a peak destination to arrive at?

_____

_____

_____

_____

_____

◆ Describe the feeling of the art of silence and the art of sound that this Sutra talks about.

_____

_____

_____

_____

_____

_____

65.
KNOW THE DELUSION TO
KNOW THE TRUTH

◆ How do you currently relate with each of the three
biggest torments—sex, money, and power?

_____

_____

_____

_____

_____

_____

- Have you ever deliberately entered a domain like one of these with the intention of learning the mechanics? If so, describe your experience. If not, what has had you avoid it?

_____

_____

_____

_____

_____

_____

- What would it be like to have mastery in those areas?

_____

_____

_____

_____

_____

_____

66.
KNOWING WHAT WE KNOW

◆ How do you usually sense into whether your next move is the right one or not?

_____

_____

_____

_____

_____

_____

◆ Have you ever experienced the lighting this Sutra talks about?

_____

_____

_____

_____

_____

_____

♦ What's an example of a time when you followed the lighting, and a time when you dismissed it?

_____

_____

_____

_____

_____

_____

TUMESCENCE

67.

DEFINING TUMESCENCE

◆ What does tumescence feel like for you in your body?

_____

_____

_____

_____

_____

_____

◆ What is an example of a time when you harnessed and
directed arousal, and a time it got stuck in your body
instead?

_____

_____

_____

68.

MECHANICS OF TUMESCENCE

◆ What is an example of an original block that you have
from your past that currently gets reactivated by
something less intense but similar? For example, you
had a parent who was very rule-based and rigid and you
often felt like you were doing it wrong or in trouble
with them. As an adult, you have a boss or authority
figure who is also that way and you end up feeling like a
kid again.

_____

_____

_____

_____

_____

- Give an example of a recent time where you experienced a random influx of energy, maybe also at work, that triggered that original accumulation of tumescence.

_____

_____

_____

_____

_____

_____

- Describe what it feels like when one of these pockets of backed-up pain gets opened.

_____

_____

_____

_____

_____

_____

◆ Describe a time when there was an activation of energy like that, but your attention was stronger than the activation, meaning you were able to stay calm when there was an urge to go into your reactivity.

_____

_____

_____

_____

_____

_____

69.

TUMESCENCE EMERGES FROM
WITHDRAWN CONSCIOUSNESS

◆ Do you feel well rested after a day of scrolling social
media, watching Netflix, etc.? What types of activities
help you to feel rested and digested?

_____

_____

_____

_____

_____

_____

- Do you tend to push really hard and effort past what your body actually can do and then crash? If so, what has you do that and why?

_____

_____

_____

_____

_____

_____

- What is an example for you of real-time digestion?

_____

_____

_____

_____

_____

_____

70.

CLIMAX CONSCIOUSNESS

◆ Describe a recent time when your tumescence built
until a "discharge" was the only way out.

_____

_____

_____

_____

_____

_____

◆ What tumescent pockets of stuck energy do you feel
like you might have?

_____

_____

_____

_____

_____

_____

◆ Have you ever had the experience of turning toward and slowly opening to tumescence instead of avoiding or discharging it?

_____

_____

_____

_____

_____

71.
PERFECTIONISM TAKES OVER
THE TUMESCENT MIND

◆ What tyrannical demands does your perfectionism
   tumescence put on you?

_____

_____

_____

_____

_____

_____

◆ How does it disconnect you from the consciousness
   that would give it relief?

_____

_____

_____

_____

_____

_____

◆ In what ways do you try to shift your external reality to produce an internal sense of safety?

_____

_____

_____

_____

_____

_____

72.

TUMESCENCE RELIES ON SCARCITY

◆ How might you penetrate your tumescent mind?

_____

_____

_____

_____

_____

_____

◆ What are the things the running voice uses to keep you
from sinking in?

_____

_____

_____

_____

_____

_____

♦ Do you have practices in your life that give you a daily opportunity to sink in?

_____

_____

_____

_____

_____

_____

ABOVE TO BELOW

73.
THE PATH TO
UNCONDITIONAL FREEDOM

◆ What are some things you consider taboo that may have
that 'nutritive concentration' this Sutra talks about?

_____

_____

_____

_____

_____

_____

◆ What is an example of something you've done the 'alchemical process' with: from pain to medicine; to administering medicine; to making medicine available for use?

_____

_____

_____

_____

_____

_____

◆ What does it mean to you to hear and see accurately into the heart of all things?

_____

_____

_____

_____

_____

_____

74.

EXALT THE BOTTOM

- What's your relationship with your body currently like? In what ways do you treat it as below you or less than?

_____

_____

_____

_____

_____

_____

- What is something you have suppressed or cut off in yourself that your body remembers?

_____

_____

_____

_____

_____

_____

◆ What is something "profane" that you actually have
reverence for?

_____

_____

_____

_____

_____

_____

75.

CASTING OUT
AND RETURNING

◆ What do you think is the perceived extra weight that we
would be told to drop off to achieve higher levels of
consciousness?

_____

_____

_____

_____

_____

_____

◆ What is it like for you in the moments that you're able to experience reality without the residue of judgment?

_____

_____

_____

_____

_____

_____

76.
EROS CALLS US
BACK HOME

◆ What do you think is our true nature?

_____

_____

_____

_____

_____

_____

◆ Describe an experience where you felt like you came
back home to Eros.

_____

_____

_____

_____

_____

_____

77.

MASTERY IN EROS
IS RELATIONAL

♦ What "credentials" do you have from having gone
through certain experiences in your life? These would
be more along the lines of street smarts from being in
the streets, versus a degree you got from a university.

_____

_____

_____

_____

_____

_____

◆ What is an experience you had that you hated at the time and came to appreciate later?

_____

_____

_____

_____

_____

_____

78.

AN EXPERIENTIAL PATH,
NOT RENUNCIATION

◆ What is a "problem" happening currently in your life
that might actually be a gaining of experience that Eros
is inviting you into?

_____

_____

_____

_____

_____

_____

◆ Where is a place in your life that you're trying to bypass the experience to just get to the deeper truth without going through the challenge of it?

_____

_____

_____

_____

_____

_____

◆ What's an obsession you're currently researching?

_____

_____

_____

_____

_____

79.

OUR GRAVITY

◆ What is an "ascendent state" that you've seen as superior to just going straight into the challenges of life?

_____

_____

_____

_____

_____

_____

◆ What's a drop of beauty you've collected that's become part of your gravity?

_____

_____

_____

80.
MASCULINE SPIRITUALITY RESTRAINS EROS

◆ Where do you apply restraint against the spontaneous communications of your body?

_____

_____

_____

_____

_____

_____

◆ Why do you think many people consider this consciousness of restraint to be more evolved?

_____

_____

_____

_____

_____

_____

◆ What does it feel like to you when your Erotic impulses
   and consciousness are in alliance?

_____

_____

_____

_____

_____

_____

81.

FEMININE SPIRITUALITY
IS ROOTED IN NATURE

◆ What are some aspects of your humanity that you see as
distractions from spirit?

_____

_____

_____

_____

_____

_____

◆ Why is woman seen as the embodiment of what will
lure man down?

_____

_____

_____

_____

_____

_____

◆ How do you feel about the idea that a woman needs to
cultivate the power to educate without punishment?

_____

_____

_____

_____

_____

82.

THE INTELLIGENCE
OF THE BODY

◆ What does it mean to you that the body is a form of
ordered and sentient intelligence?

_____

_____

_____

_____

_____

_____

◆ What do you think life is like from the body's
perspective?

_____

_____

_____

_____

_____

_____

◆ Where is a place that you closed to something intense, uncertain, or unfamiliar that you blamed on your body but was actually your consciousness closing?

_____

_____

_____

_____

_____

_____

◆ Why does the mind have a hard time surrendering to the body?

_____

_____

_____

_____

_____

_____

- What does it feel like when your consciousness descends down into your own body?

_____

_____

_____

_____

_____

_____

83.

THE ULTIMATE CON GAME

◆ In what ways do you think of your body as inferior to consciousness?

_____

_____

_____

_____

_____

_____

◆ In what ways is the mind quite fragile?

_____

_____

_____

◆ In what ways does your own mind coerce you?

◆ How does the idea that the mind makes the body
dependent on it sit with you?

◆ This Sutra compares the mind making the body dependent on it to the US congratulating itself for including Native Americans or for extending generosity to slaves. What other examples of this do you see in the world?

_____

_____

_____

_____

_____

_____

◆ How has your mind used your body as a tool?

_____

_____

_____

_____

_____

_____

84.

HOW THE MIND ACHIEVES JOY

- What does simple connection and intimacy with the body look like for you?

  _____

  _____

  _____

  _____

  _____

  _____

- Why do you think listening is one of the main ways for the mind to stay tethered to the body?

  _____

  _____

  _____

_____

_____

_____

◆ What do you think it would be like if your mind no longer checked out of your body?

_____

_____

_____

_____

_____

_____

◆ Why do you think the body is so specific and precise with exactly what it wants?

_____

_____

_____

_____

_____

_____

◆ How is complaint a form of bragging?

_____

_____

_____

_____

_____

_____

◆ What are the main ways your mind asks your body to
   leave the present moment?

_____

_____

_____

_____

_____

_____

85.

WHAT IS UNSPEAKABLE IN THE ASCENDENT IS HONORABLE IN THE DESCENDENT

◆ How does sneaking darkness give it a bad reputation?

_____

_____

_____

_____

_____

_____

- What is your relationship to the involuntary currently like?

_____

_____

_____

_____

_____

_____

86.

EXPOSE INNOCENCE

♦ What do you think it would be like if the power of your involuntary subsumed your rational mind?

_____

_____

_____

_____

_____

_____

♦ Why does exposing yourself make it so that projections can't adhere?

_____

_____

_____

_____

_____

_____

PLAY

87.

EROS FINDS PLAY,
NOT PROBLEMS

- What are two specific ways that you notice your mind tends to seek problems?

  _____

  _____

  _____

  _____

  _____

  _____

- What's an example of a cultural identity forming from a series of problems and solutions?

  _____

  _____

_____

_____

_____

_____

◆ Have you ever felt shame for thinking something wasn't a problem that many people around you did find a problem? And if so, describe the experience.

_____

_____

_____

_____

_____

◆ What would it be like to not see discomfort as a problem? How might you then express?

_____

_____

_____

_____

_____

◆ What are two ways you see yourself use "problems" to "hold to the side of the pool"?

_____

_____

_____

_____

_____

_____

◆ How might your life be different if it was organized around creativity rather than problems?

_____

_____

_____

_____

_____

_____

◆ What would it be like to shift gears from the series of questions the rational mind asks (that the Sutra references) into those Eros-based questions where you are more intimately engaging from a totally different part of you?

_____

_____

_____

_____

_____

_____

88.

A CONGRUENT MIND
SEEKS TO LOSE WELL

◆ How does this Sutra use the word 'congruence'? What does it mean? What does it show us in this context?

_____

_____

_____

_____

_____

_____

- Do you currently feel like you have to grip strongly to
  your opinions and ideas, or do you feel able to allow
  them to be pushed against and tested for truth?

_____

_____

_____

_____

_____

_____

- Have you ever had an experience where you got to have
  a connected wrestle with someone until a truth was
  revealed, which brought you closer? If so, describe the
  experience.

_____

_____

_____

_____

_____

_____

ETHICS

89.

LAWLESS LAWS

◆ Currently, do you feel like your life is constructed more from the rational or from internal structures?

_____

_____

_____

_____

_____

_____

◆ What is one specific way you can see that the Erotic does not conform to assumptions or predictability?

_____

_____

_____

90.

EVOLUTION IS
EROTIC MORALITY

◆ What does the sentence, "In the conception of Eros
there is no such thing as sin," bring up for you?

_____

_____

_____

_____

_____

_____

◆ How does punishment seem easier than evolving the
unevolved, in ourselves and in others?

_____

_____

_____

_____

_____

_____

◆ What is something in yourself or in another that you've longed to forgive but haven't given yourself permission to?

_____

_____

_____

_____

_____

_____

91.

EROTIC ETHICS

♦ In what ways does this Sutra relate to the perfection
section of the Principles Sutras?

_____

_____

_____

_____

_____

_____

♦ How are you at matching funds with people? Do you
tend to withhold support or want more for people than
they want for themselves?

_____

_____

_____

_____

_____

_____

_____

◆ Where in your life do you feel you could take more personal responsibility for your experience?

_____

_____

_____

_____

_____

◆ What is one place in your life where you could lean in more, become more intimate with, and practice in?

_____

_____

_____

_____

_____

NOTES

NOTES

NOTES

NOTES

NOTES

NOTES

NOTES

THE EROS SUTRAS VOLUMES

VOLUME 1
PRINCIPLES

◆

VOLUME 2
TUMESCENCE

◆

VOLUME 3
ORGASMIC MEDITATION

◆

VOLUME 4
RELATIONSHIP

◆

VOLUME 5
LIBERATION & JUSTICE